Top-Heavy America

Business Model
for a New Age of the
American Employee

A Little Book By:

Paeti Gustav Xaviers

At Sun:
TWiNKLe, TWiNKLe, EyeS at SUN...

Twinkle, Twinkle, little stars,
How I WONDER whose you Are's,
Up Above the Sky so High,
Just Like GOD,
In mine eye.

- My First Poem

Paeti Gustav Xaviers, Age 5

About Paeti

Paeti was born during the early nighttime hours of a cold New Year's Eve in 1953 as Patricia (Patti) Jane Markow. She was raised in the bustling city of Elizabeth, New Jersey, and graduated from the public school system in 1971. After briefly attending college post Battin High School graduation, she entered the work force. In her early 20's she started her career in the field of Mortgage Banking.

By the time she was 28 years old, she was a National Award Winning junior executive with a mid-sized New Jersey Mortgage Banking Corporation. Within a few years, she would become the first woman to be elected to the Board of Governors of the New Jersey Mortgage Bankers Association. During that same time, she became engaged to marry a prominent attorney and the love of her existence.

Paeti's promising life was abruptly struck down, for the simple reason that she was a possible abuser of marijuana. Due to erratic behavior, causing the concern of others, she became disabled from holding her position of employment and lost her fiance. She was diagnosed with schizophrenia. Years of denial and disbelief caused her to lash out at anyone who tried to "help" her. She suffered through the humiliation and indignities of multiple involuntary captivities in psychiatric wards. In an effort to run away from it all, she fell from a world endowed by an up and coming career and a decent income to the ranks of the impoverished, poorly surviving on welfare.

By the time of her early 40's, she lived in a tiny, dingy room of a rooming house in a small resort town on the Jersey shore. A life alone and moderately frightening woke her each morning and haunted her each night until a serious altercation with another resident of the dilapidated housing unit landed Paeti trouble with the police and incarcerated in jail. She was found "Not Guilty."

The years and the trauma gradually passed as Paeti resigned herself to possibly a lifetime remainder of unnecessary phychiatric medication and professional mental health treatment. Yet still determined to try to prove that there was nothing incompetent about herself, she returned to college. She graduated from an accredited University in 2009 with a 4.0 GPA and an A.A. degree in Law.

Living a newly serene and stable life in sunny Florida, making ends meet financially by earning small sums from working at home, she authored numerous articles and small books. She also taught herself web design in addition to causing a piece of jewelry, inspired from her "pot head" days and called "The Xaviers Cross,' to become a reality. She enjoys solitude, writing, rocking chairs, her computer and listening to soft rock or classical music.

Paeti has authored books under pennames: Paeti Gustav Xaviers and Patti Gustav Xaviers, and also under the name of Patti Markow.

Other Books by This Author:

Without Recourse: Misdiagnosed Mentally Ill
There's No Such Thing as "Medical" Marijuana
The Spirit Cries
Penning Profits with HubPages
Sure-Win Baccarat
Sure-Win Baccarat II
Sure-Win Baccarat III
Sure-Win Baccarat IV
Sure-Win Baccarat V
Custom Website Coding
Official Record: God is Love
No One Asks to be Born
A Sound Theory
The Divinity Creations
The Incarnation
Fat, Fat You At!
On Mating, Marrying and Multi-Orgasmic Bliss
The Church of Xaviers: An Xaviers Collection
A Mormon Testimony (Pre-Baptism)
O Holy Smoke: Ritualistic Smoking of Tobacco
The Spirit Must Die
Consummation Worship: "What What You Eat!"
A Routine for Healty, Happy, Affordable Living

Top-Heavy America

PLEASE LISTEN!

The lives of millions of Americans are at stake. What I would like to bring to your attention is a solution to a crisis, which I sent to my local legislators without one iota of response. I believe this matter is critical to insuring that the Human Rights of all people employed by commercial entities are not violated. Passage of legislation would not only greatly improve the financial well being of America's employees, but also have an incredibly positive affect on our Nation's economy.

I was meditating upon the enigma in the reality which constitutes the current system of life...to find what must be the "bug," or "unintentional error," in the logic that ANY HUMAN BEING, regardless of innate, acquired or accidental abilities and/or disabilities, should be literally "doomed" to a life of financial troubles and hardships.

The conclusion of my thoughts generated a legal argument that relates to business and human rights law. The circumstance and logic applied in the draw of the conclusion are already published and of record in a little book entitled: "No One Asks to be Born...The Endless Enigma of Reality: Resolved" by author Patti Markow (available on Amazon).

Although I believe my argument is valid, I am not a lawyer. The issues it involves must be debated by knowledgeable legal minds in order to confirm the validity.

Should it be determined that the argument is valid, may I please propose the introduction of legislation in order to clarify in the law the extended words necessary to insure true and just respect of an individual's human rights, specifically as they relate to employment, and the illegality in the exploitation of a commercial entity's human resources.

THE CONCLUSION:

"It is ILLEGAL for the owner(s) of any commercial entity,

including any business or corporation, that employs HUMAN RESOURCES to in ANY WAY, actual OR implied, claim OWNERSHIP of that percentage of the entity's value that is attributable to human resources. "Implied" would include the claim of any soul right to reap the benefit(s) of that value. That would constitute a direct or indirect OWNERSHIP of HUMAN BEINGS.

In order that the employment of human resources NOT be constituted or construed as

HUMAN EXPLOITATION, a percentage of the NET PROFITS, equal to the percentage of the entity's value that is attributable to human resources, MUST BE distributed to those HUMAN EMPLOYEES that ARE the entity's asset: Human Resources. This percentage of the net profits must be distributed to the human resources IN ADDITION TO the employee's agreed upon "rate of regular compensation" and NOT claimed as belonging exclusively to the owner(s) of the entity.

The agreed upon "rate of regular compensation" must only be construed to be the equivalent of a "contract retainer," assuring the entity that the associated job will in fact be performed, REGARDLESS of the amount of any profits that may be earned by the entity, and NOT as the final "fixed and full" amount of compensation owed to and earned by the human resources. Human resources MUST be compensated the full and actual dollar amount that their work is worth, as determined by the percentage of the net profits that is equal to the percentage of the value of the entity that is attributable to human resources."

PLEASE LISTEN! The foregoing is a sincere effort "fix" that "bug" that leaves SO MANY HONEST AND COOPERATIVE individuals "doomed" to an inappropriate life of financial struggles, hardship and possibly poverty when it should be INSURED by the laws of this great country that NO ONE'S HUMAN RIGHTS will in any way be violated.

Top-Heavy America

Free enterprise is what makes America great. Businesses flourish and create a wealth that is the backbone of our economy. Yet, with all of this wealth, the majority of Americans struggle to afford a decent and respectable life for themselves. Many Americans seem even doomed to exist within the ranks of poverty, regardless of their willingness to work.

The problem lies in what I call the "wealth flow." While the majority of the wealth lies in profit-wielding businesses, endowing the business owners and stockholders, the typical employee is contracted to a salary that is independent of the business' income. The wealth of the business flows only to the owners/stockholders and not to the employees who perform the work that generates that wealth. America is "top-heavy."

Human resources is the most valuable asset a business can claim. Certainly, it is appreciable as employees' career paths create them to be more knowledgeable, capable and efficient in their positions. Yet, regardless of the dollar value of this appreciation, typically reflected in an increase in the profits that a business can generate, the employees' rewards often culminate in a minor, "cost-of-living" increase in wages earned.

There is nothing wrong with a business' profits flowing to business owners and stockholders. There is nothing wrong with business owners and stockholders receiving a return on their investments. But an employee invests his time and talent, an important aspect of his life and existence, into the creation of a business' income. The crucial question is "Why does not a fair share of the profits that the employees 'slave' to generate not enrich the employees' financial condition as well as it does the business' owners and stockholders?"

Rightfully, it should. And it should not be just in "Christmas Bonuses." Although the current and prominent business structure contracts an employee to a fixed, regular rate of compensation, this fixed, regular amount should be considered as only a "contract retainer," insuring the business entity that the particular job employed will be performed regardless of the entity's profit or loss. The employees truly have a right to that portion of a business' profits proportionate to the percentage of the asset value human resources is to the enterprise.

The crux of much of the economic problems that America

experiences could be in the lack of stimulation. Simply, if America's employees were to receive the just and full amount of compensation that their work and toil is worth to businesses, more money would be flowing into the hands of consumers. The more money consumers have, logically, the more money they will spend. Consumers would spend their money toward the income of businesses. The income of businesses would flow to the owners/stockholders and a just and fair share of that income will flow back into the hands of consumers (the employees), in addition to their contracted rate of regular compensation. The circle of cash flow would continually stimulate the economy and would create a standard of general economic "good health."

The Xaviers Business Model

The Xaviers Business Model is equivalent to the business model that is prevalent in modern society. The business entity would be organized in accordance with the legal standards applicable at the time of organization. The business will establish its owners and open itself to share purchase by stockholders, if the business so desires and is qualified. The exception to the "standard" business model that distinguishes the Xaviers Business Model lies in the contracting of workers, or employees.

As is the norm, a position of employment that is applied for by a man or woman, will promise a regular rate of compensation appropriate to the degree of responsibility and qualifications of the prospective employee. However, once contracted, the regular rate of compensation will constitute only the "contract retainer." In addition to his/her regular rate of wages earned, the employee will also, within the employment contract, be entitled to a just and fair share of the business' profits. This just and fair share is to be determined proportionate to the percentage of the value of the business enterprise that is attributable to the business' human resources. The employee will receive an equal share of this percentage of the NET profits, which percentage of the net profits will be divided equally among all members of the business' asset that is constituted by its employees.

To put it simply, if human

resources constitutes 74% to 96% of any corporations value, then 74% to 96% of the corporation's net profits belong to the employees...not the owners and/or stockholders. Each employee should receive an equal share of that percentage of the net profits. If the employees do not receive their just and fair share, the ACTUAL VALUE that their work is worth, then it is equivalent to exploitation of the human resources. Further, a business enterprise cannot claim ownership of the percentage of the entity that is attributable to human resources. This would illegally constitute a direct or indirect ownership of human beings.

Let's use an example:

Sam & Joe establish a corporation called "Lawn Cutters" and buy a lawn mower for $225. Sam & Joe don't want to cut lawns themselves, so the lawn mower just sits there, depreciating. The value of the corporation is a depreciating $225.

Sam & Joe decide to hire Ralph for $10/hr. to do the lawn cutting and plan to charge $60 for every lawn that is cut. Ralph uses the company lawn mower. In one day, 8 hours, Ralph cuts 5 lawns and earns $300 for the company.

Out of the money earned, the "overhead" is deducted: $80 for Ralph's salary and let's allow $10 for depreciation of the lawn mower. The total net profit was $210. Now the value of the corporation is $225 (lawn mower) plus $210 (net profit):

$435.00.

The $210 is the value added
to the corporation by the
HUMAN RESOURCES (Ralph).
$210 represents 48.27% of the
corporation's value that Sam &
Joe CAN'T LEGALLY claim
ownership of: it's human. That
means 48.27% of the net profits
they ALSO can't claim
ownership of: it belongs to the
human resource. So Ralph
should get an additional $101.37,
which is 48.27% of the net
profits.

Sam & Joe just made $108.63 from the depreciating lawn mower that they own and as a return for their contribution of ingenuity and capital. Ralph made $181.37, certainly a better day's earnings than just his salary of $80 and the TRUE VALUE of what his work was worth. Sam & Joe are happy. Ralph is happy. And it was all done fairly.

The way corporations work now, Sam & Joe would earn $210 from their depreciating lawn mower and Ralph would earn only his $80. This is NOT just nor a fair way of compensating an employee, considering the TRUE VALUE of the work that was performed.

Adoption of the Xaviers Model

Adopting the Xaviers Business Model into American economic life would have, obviously, tremendous impact. The American worker would be earning a more just and fair income for the work he/she performs. This would, in most cases, mean an increase in the dollar amount of wages earned. More Americans would be able to experience the "American Dream" of home ownership and the economic stimulus would be experienced in all other aspects of our economy. A "top-heavy" economy would be brought into a more just and fair balance.

Of course, there is another consideration. There would be less profit at the disposal of business owners and stockholders. Still, I would certainly hope that the heart of business owners and stockholders is not ruled by greed. Unfortunately, it is a fact that at least some greed plays a part. Although voluntary mass adoption of the Xaviers Model by American businesses would be a nice gesture on the businesses' parts, legislation to insure that human resources are not directly or indirectly "owned" and not exploited will probably most likely have to be enacted.

Once again, the following is the verbiage of the legislation proposed:

"It is ILLEGAL for the owner(s) of any commercial entity, including any business or corporation, that employs HUMAN RESOURCES to in ANY WAY, actual OR implied, claim OWNERSHIP of that percentage of the entity's value that is attributable to human resources. "Implied" would include the claim of any soul right to reap the benefit(s) of that value. That would constitute a direct or indirect OWNERSHIP of HUMAN BEINGS.

In order that the employment of human resources NOT be constituted or construed as HUMAN EXPLOITATION, a percentage of the NET PROFITS, equal to the percentage of the entity's value that is attributable to human resources, MUST BE distributed to those HUMAN EMPLOYEES that ARE the entity's asset: Human Resources. This percentage of the net profits must be distributed to the human resources IN ADDITION TO the employee's agreed upon "rate of regular compensation" and NOT claimed as belonging exclusively to the owner(s) of the entity.

 The agreed upon "rate of regular compensation" must only be construed to be the equivalent of a "contract retainer," assuring the entity that the associated job will in fact be performed, REGARDLESS of the amount of any profits that may be earned by the entity, and NOT as the final "fixed and full" amount of compensation owed to and earned by the human resources. Human resources MUST be compensated the full and actual dollar amount that their work is worth, as determined by the percentage of the net profits that is equal to the percentage of the value of the entity that is attributable to human resources."

AMerica NeedS tHe XavierS ModeL

America and the American worker need the Xaviers Business Model to be adopted as soon as feasibly possible. America needs the economic stimulation and the American worker needs the insurance that he/she is not doomed to a lifestyle that could never improve or that poverty is the end-all to everything.

The American worker must,

without exception, be
compensated the just and fair
value that his/her work is worth
to a business and not be strictly
contracted to a fixed income.
His/her income should fluctuate
proportionately to the
fluctuations of a business' net
profits, without the fear of losing
all compensation, considering the
insurance of the employment
contract retainer.

Businesses need to consider the
true value of their human
resources and not exploit it to
greed's end for the sake of

monetary profit. Human resources is the most valuable asset a business can claim. Those employees that constitute the human resources should be respected as so valuable and compensated for their investment of such a substantial portion of their lives with a more just and fair promise of a percentage of net profits, in addition to some regular and fixed sum.

America cannot afford to remain in an economic situation that is riddled by imbalance. The scale can be tilted to level and the financial well-being of many, if not most, Americans can be moved from traumatizing to dream with the cooperation of everyone involved in business activity.

www.ingramcontent.com/pod-product-compliance
Lightning Source LLC
Chambersburg PA
CBHW071007180526
45168CB00003B/1323